EVERYBODY HAS A BODY

For Calvin: You inspire everything I do.
For all the children who feel different: You are seen and loved. —M. J. E.

For my body: I love you, and thanks. —L. T.

A Feiwel and Friends Book
An imprint of Macmillan Publishing Group, LLC
120 Broadway, New York, NY 10271 • mackids.com

Our books may be purchased in bulk for promotional, educational, or business use.
Please contact your local bookseller or the Macmillan Corporate and Premium Sales Department
at (800) 221-7945 ext. 5442 or by email at MacmillanSpecialMarkets@macmillan.com.

Library of Congress Control Number: 2022920041

First edition, 2023
Book design by Aram Kim
Art is created digitally.
Feiwel and Friends logo designed by Filomena Tuosto
Printed in China by RR Donnelley Asia Printing Solutions Ltd., Dongguan City, Guangdong Province

ISBN 978-1-250-85444-5
1 3 5 7 9 10 8 6 4 2

EVERYBODY HAS A BODY

MOLLI JACKSON EHLERT

illustrated by LORIAN TU

Feiwel and Friends

New York

Everybody has a body.

When we're born,

as we grow,

our bodies take us
through the world.

As we move

and feel,

and play

our bodies are part
of who we are.

Everybody has a body.

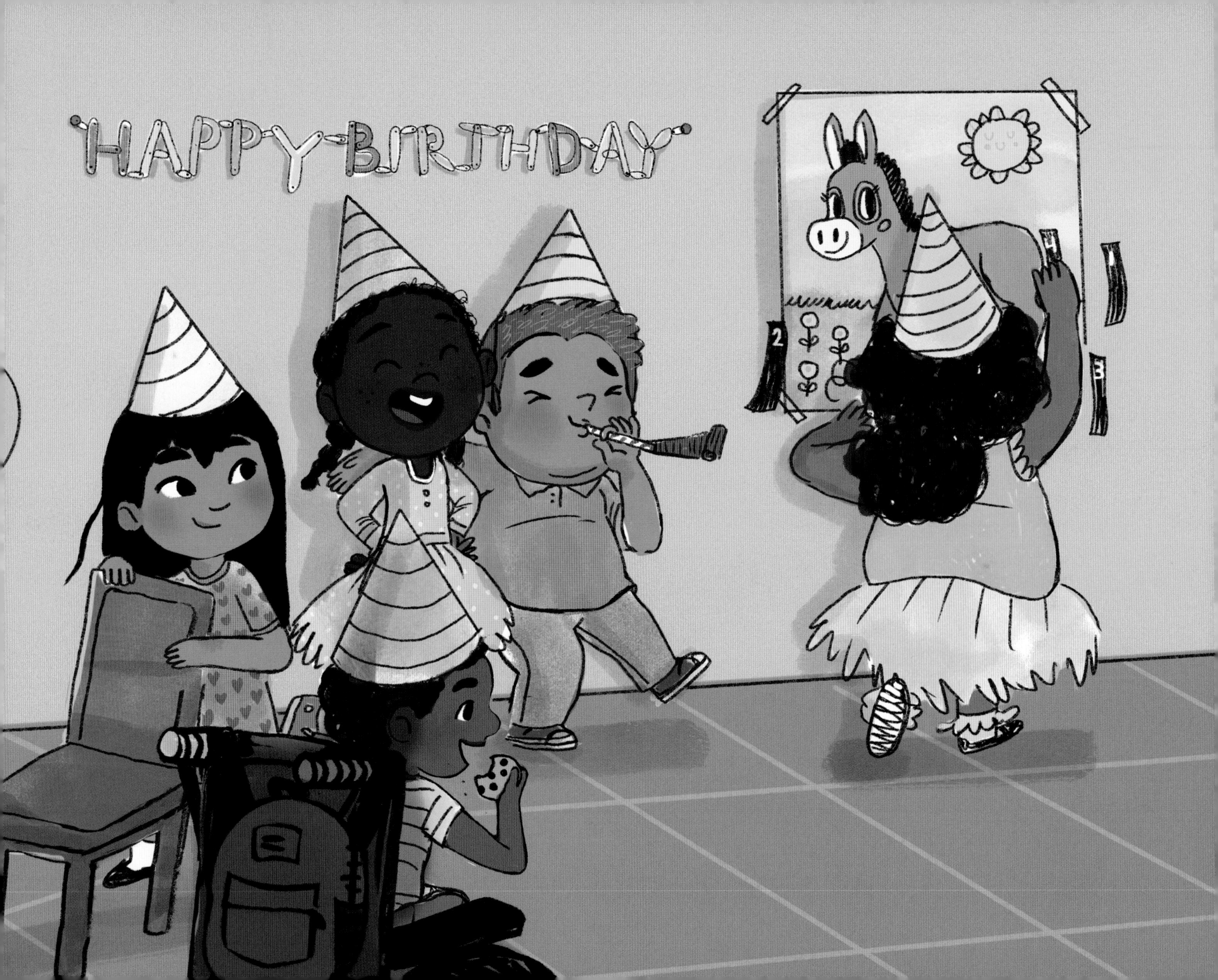
HAPPY BIRTHDAY
2
3
4

Bodies look different ways.
Some are short, some are tall.
Some are small, some are large.

Some are different colors,
some are different shapes.

Everybody has a body.

Bodies have different needs.

Some move in different ways,
some see in different ways.

Some talk in different ways,
some think in different ways.

Some just got here,
some have been here a long time.

Everybody has a body.

Bodies do different things.

Some adventure outdoors,

some adventure indoors.

Some create life,

some save lives.

Some make change,

some make art.

Everybody has a body.

Bodies feel different ways.
Some feel good playing,
some feel good resting.

Some feel hairy,
some feel bumpy.

Some feel strong,
some feel flexible.

Everybody has a body.

Your body is your body.
It doesn't look like anyone else's.
It doesn't feel like anyone else's.

It does things that only your body can do.
And those differences make you you.

Everybody has a body.

What is body neutrality?

Body neutrality means simply accepting your body—it's neither good nor bad, it's just the way it is! You don't need to love your body, but it's important to respect and recognize the hard work your body does.

So, how do you practice body neutrality? Here are five ways!

1. Think about what your body does for you.

Do you love to sing? Your body allows you to make music by using your vocal cords! Do you love trying new foods? Your body allows you to taste and enjoy all types of food! Think about how your body lets you interact with the world around you.

2. Allow yourself to just feel *meh*.

You won't always feel amazing. Sometimes your body will ache. Sometimes your body will be tired. When you don't feel great, be kind and gentle to yourself. Remember that taking care of your body sometimes means letting it rest!

3. Accept that perfect doesn't exist.

Nobody is perfect, and no body is perfect. All of us are human. We make mistakes, we have our flaws. Let yourself enjoy life, and embrace the differences and the things that make us unique.

4. Think of your body as a house.

Your body is a home. It protects your organs so you can live. That's impressivel No matter what your body looks like, the most important thing it does is keep you alive. Think about how cool that is!

5. Above all, remember you are more than your body.

The kindness you show others and the joy you bring to their lives mean more than your body ever will. The impact you make on the world will last longer than the way your body looks. Your body is constantly changing; it doesn't look today how it looked a year ago. Who you *are* is more interesting and important than your body ever could be.